WHO CREATED THE PLYMOUTH COLONY?

US HISTORY 3RD GRADE

CHILDREN'S AMERICAN HISTORY

Baby Professor

EDUCATION KIDS

In this book, we're going to talk about who established the Plymouth Colony. So, let's get right to it!

The men and women who came to America were often looking for a way to escape the persecution they were experiencing in their homeland. In 1620, a group of English settlers left their native England for a new life in America. They were the Pilgrims and they were risking their lives to obtain religious freedom.

Pilgrims

Cathedral in England

WHO WERE THE PILGRIMS?

The Pilgrims didn't want to be part of the Church of England. They wanted the right to worship exactly as they wished. In England, they had been called "Separatists" because they were separating from the ways that the Church of England believers followed.

At times they had been imprisoned and sometimes even persecuted for their beliefs. There were other reasons to journey to the New World as well. Some of the Pilgrims wanted to travel to the New World for adventure and for the thrill of a different type of life than they were used to in England.

I. Luyken.

TIME TO SET SAIL

At this point in time, there was only one way to get across the Atlantic Ocean. It was a treacherous journey by ship for thousands of miles. The Pilgrims were very brave to even attempt it. They set sail on two different ships. One of the ships was called the Speedwell and the other was known as the Mayflower.

The Mayflower at sea

Unfortunately, the Speedwell wasn't true to its name. Soon after they left port, the ship sprang a major leak. The Pilgrims had to turn around and go back. Once they were back, they decided to crowd everyone on the Mayflower.

They were able to get 102 of the group on the ship, but were forced to leave some of the Speedwell travelers behind. To operate the ship there were about 25 crewmen on board as well. The ship was about 106 feet in length and only 25 feet wide. It was a very tight space for so many people.

The Speedwell at sea

THE MAYFLOWER VOYAGE

The long voyage to travel across the Atlantic was very dangerous. The situation was made worse by the fact that the ship was crowded with too many people. Lack of fresh water became an issue during the journey. Many of the Pilgrims became ill and two people perished on the way. Raging storms rocked the ship to the point where one of the main beams cracked.

The situation was looking grim and the Pilgrims considered turning around and heading back to England, but they didn't want to give up their chance for religious freedom. They discussed the situation and decided to continue. After eight long weeks at sea, they finally saw land on the horizon. They had arrived in the New World!

Landing of the Pilgrims

THE MAYFLOWER COMPACT

When they set foot in what is now called New England, the Pilgrims knew that they would need some type of plan to provide the basis for a new government. They worked together to create a document to list the way they wanted their community to operate. Today that document is known as the Mayflower Compact. The Mayflower Compact stated the following:

- The citizens of the colony pledged their loyalty to the King of England.

Mayflower Compact

- They believed in Christianity and would serve God as they worshipped.
- They would also demonstrate their Christian beliefs in the way they treated their community.
- They would create laws that they felt were fair and have standards for justice.
- They would always consider issues with a focus on the benefit of the overall colony and all the people living in it. In other words, the welfare of the community would be more important than the welfare of an individual.

Forty-one men signed the document. At that time, women didn't sign legal documents. They also designated that they wanted John Carver to be their first governor.

PLYMOUTH COLONY

When the Pilgrims first landed on what is now known as New England's coast, they searched for a location that they felt would be a good spot for a village. Eventually, they decided to choose land that was on the southern coast of what is now the state of Massachusetts.

It was a complete coincidence that "Plymouth" had been named years earlier after the city in England that they had sailed from. The harbor at Plymouth was relatively calm so it was a good place to dock the Mayflower. There was a freshwater river nearby and the lands were flat and suitable for planting crops. They began to build some structures to establish their new colony of Plymouth.

Mayflower Replica

A DIFFICULT WINTER

When the Pilgrims arrived in America, it was already November and they were not prepared for the harsh New England winter that was about to begin. The men got together and very quickly built a common house for the community.

Then they started to construct smaller dwellings to house each family. For quite some time, a group of people slept on the ship.

The winter was devastating. Many people became ill and died that first winter season. There was a time when only six of the men were able-bodied enough to continue construction on the buildings.

William Bradford

By winter's end, 55 of the Pilgrims had died, leaving only 47 of the original settlers. Even their governor, John Carver, passed away in the spring. The settlers appointed William Bradford to govern the colony. He was to remain their governor for thirty years.

THE WAMPANOAG

There were Native Americans living in the Plymouth area when the Pilgrims arrived. These tribes were known as the Wampanoag. Their chief, who was named Massasoit, befriended the Pilgrims. He signed a treaty of peace with them and the two groups traded goods.

Massasoit

Squanto

In their group was a man called Squanto. Squanto had been to Europe and while he was there he had learned to speak some English. He helped the Pilgrims to stay alive by teaching them basic survival skills.

He showed them the way to properly plant corn. He also taught them hunting and fishing skills and techniques for surviving the harsh winter weather. Without Squanto's help, the Pilgrims would more than likely not have survived.

Thanksgiving

THE FIRST THANKSGIVING

After their first harvest in the year 1621, Governor Bradford proclaimed that they should celebrate. They asked the local Native Americans who had helped them, to share in their feast.

T H A N
G I

Two years later there was a severe drought and that year they began to call the holiday "Thanksgiving" in honor of their gratitude both for the rain that finally came, and for the fact that they had survived.

FASCINATING FACTS ABOUT THE PILGRIMS

- The "Separatists" sometimes called the other members of the colony that didn't share their religious beliefs "Strangers."
- William Bradford wrote in his journal about the events at Plymouth and this is why we have a record of what took place there.

Plymouth Rock

- There's a rock where the Pilgrims supposedly landed that's called "Plymouth Rock." Many tourists have taken pieces of the rock for souvenirs and now the rock is only one-third of its original size.

- Some of the Pilgrims had been to America before their trip on the Mayflower. One of the passengers was a man named Stephen Hopkins. He had tried to settle in Jamestown a decade before.

Stephen Hopkins' House

The Tempest

However, his ship crashed at the Bermuda coast and he and other passengers were stuck there until they were rescued. Shakespeare's play called "The Tempest" was based on this dramatic event. Eventually, Hopkins returned to England and joined the Mayflower passengers.

Cape Cod

- The Pilgrims didn't land at Plymouth to begin with. They first landed at Cape Cod in the location that is now called Provincetown. If you look at a map, you will see that this piece of land extends out into the Atlantic and Cape Cod Bay is between Provincetown and Plymouth.

Hudson River

The Pilgrims wanted to settle near the Hudson River and had planned to create farms north of where New York City stands today. However, with winter approaching, the weather was stormy and they couldn't continue north. Their supplies were getting thin so they had to make a decision. They chose to continue across Cape Cod Bay and settle in Plymouth instead.

SUMMARY

The Pilgrims came to America in search of religious freedom because they didn't want to worship according to the beliefs of the Church of England. They arrived on the southern coastline of what is today the state of Massachusetts after a perilous journey across the Atlantic Ocean in a ship called the Mayflower. They set foot on land in winter and had to quickly build housing.

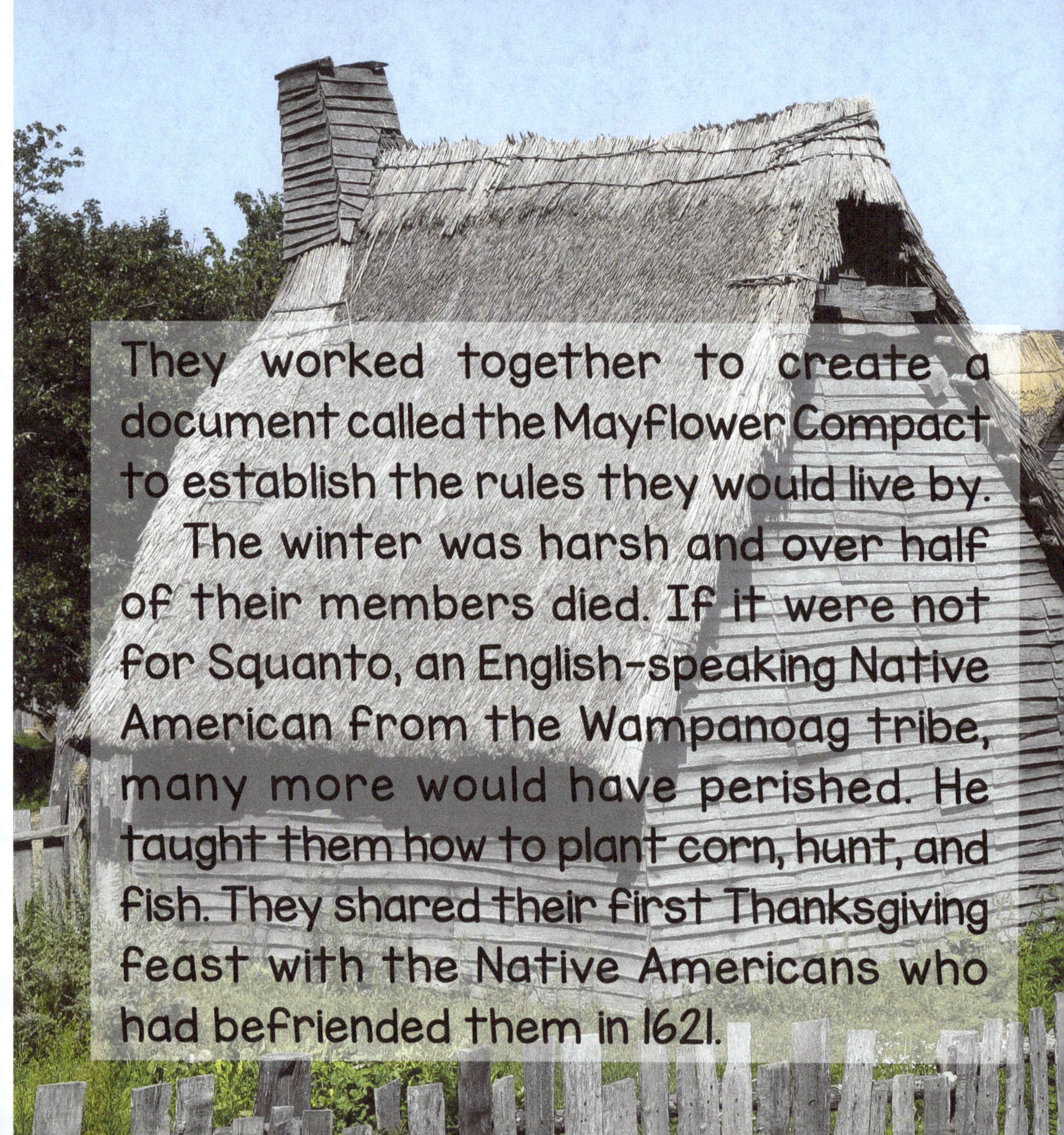
They worked together to create a document called the Mayflower Compact to establish the rules they would live by.
The winter was harsh and over half of their members died. If it were not for Squanto, an English-speaking Native American from the Wampanoag tribe, many more would have perished. He taught them how to plant corn, hunt, and fish. They shared their first Thanksgiving feast with the Native Americans who had befriended them in 1621.

Wampanoag Village

Awesome! Now that you know more about the Plymouth Colony you may want to find out more about life in the colonies more than a century later during the Revolutionary War in the Baby Professor book *The Daily Life of Colonists during the Revolutionary War.*

Visit
BABY PROFESSOR
EDUCATION KIDS
www.BabyProfessorBooks.com
to download Free Baby Professor eBooks
and view our catalog of new and exciting
Children's Books

www.ingramcontent.com/pod-product-compliance
Lightning Source LLC
Chambersburg PA
CBHW080806120726
48001CB00009B/2864